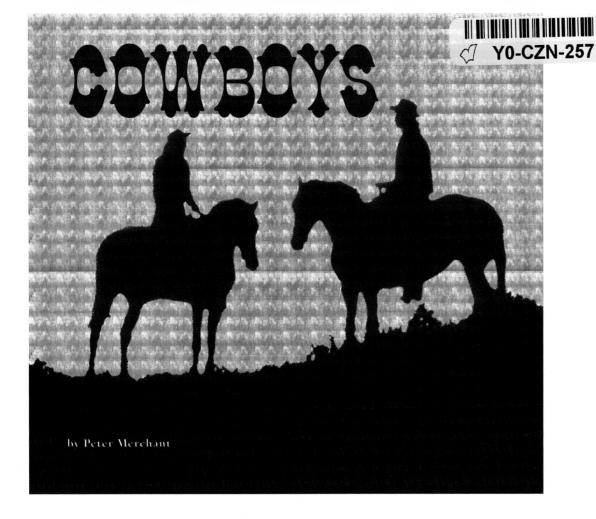

COWBOYS

by Peter Merchant

SCHOLASTIC INC.
New York   Toronto   London   Auckland   Sydney
Mexico City   New Delhi   Hong Kong   Buenos Aires

Developed by Kirchoff/Wohlberg, Inc., in cooperation with Scholastic Inc.
Credits appear on the inside back cover, which constitutes an extension of this copyright page.
Copyright © 2002 by Scholastic Inc.
All rights reserved.   Published by Scholastic Inc.   Printed in the U.S.A.
ISBN 0-439-35103-0
SCHOLASTIC and associated logos and designs are trademarks
and/or registered trademarks of Scholastic Inc.
2 3 4 5 6 7 8 9 10   14   09 08 07 06 05 04 03

What were the first cowboys really like? The real cowboys of the Old West were tough. They worked hard. They got up before dawn and worked all day. They slept only a few hours a night. On the trail, they slept out in the open. If it rained, they and their blankets got wet. They had no days off.

Their job was herding cattle and driving them along a trail. They had no real home. They sang songs to their cattle but didn't have much to say to each other. They were quiet men.

The first cowboys had cattle that came from Spain. So did the horses they rode. You might say that the very first cowboy was Spanish. His name was Coronado. He drove 500 cattle to what is now the northern part of Mexico. There was a lot of land and few people there. That was in the 1500s, about 500 years ago.

As time passed, other cowboys followed Coronado's trail. They drove cattle into what is now Texas. Spanish cowboys invented what being a cowboy was.

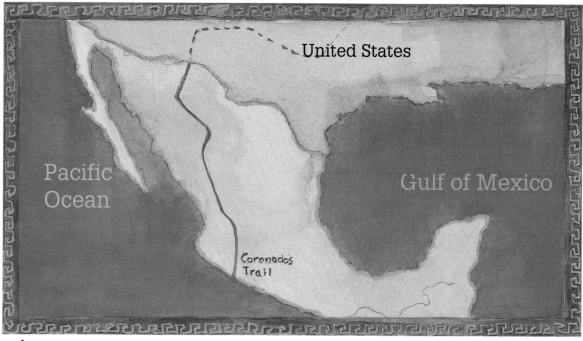

United States

Pacific Ocean

Gulf of Mexico

Coronados Trail

In fact, the English word *cowboy* means the same as the Spanish word *vaquero*. (*Vaquero* comes from *vaca*, the Spanish word for cow.) Another English word for cowboy, *buckeroo*, is just a way of saying *vaquero*.

Spanish cowboys were the first to herd and rope cattle. The cattle they roped and herded roamed free. These cattle lived all over the range, since there were no fences. They searched for food and hid in the bushes. They were tough, skinny animals with long horns.

Many of these cattle got away from the vaqueros and became wild. By 1836, there were six wild longhorn cattle for every Texan! They were as common as buffaloes.

The vaqueros also invented these things:

- **cowboy boots**, which have higher heels than other boots;
- **cowboy hats** (sombreros), which protect cowboys from sun and rain;
- **chaps**, which cowboys wear over their pants to protect their legs;

- **bandannas**, which are cloths worn around the neck;
- **lariats**, long ropes with loops on the ends for catching cattle and horses;
- **saddle horns**, the parts of saddles where the lariats go after the animal gets roped;
- **corrals**, small, fenced-in areas for animals;
- **ranches**, the home-base for a cattle business. In the Old West, a ranch included a main house, a bunk house, a corral, and lots of land.

A number of years later, in 1845, Texas became a part of the United States. Running wild through the state were 300,000 cattle. The Texans took over where the Mexicans left off. They rounded up these wild cattle into herds and sold them in the eastern and northern cities.

If there had been railroads in Texas, the Texans could have just rounded up the cattle and put them on a train. There were no trains in Texas then. So Texas cowboys had to make trails on horseback. They had to "drive" the cattle north the hard way.

United States

Pacific Ocean

Atlantic Ocean

Shawnee Trail
Western Trail
Goodnight-Loving Trail
Chisholm Trail

Gulf of Mexico

Mexico

Before a "cattle drive" could start, several things had to happen. First, cowboys went on a "cow hunt." The cowboys rode across the Texas prairie looking for a wild herd. After they found one, the cowboys would cause stampedes.

A stampede is when a herd runs out of control. The cowboys would ride with the stampede until the cattle got tired and stopped. This took all day and night sometimes. Then the cowboys would rope and "brand" them.

Branding was the way a ranch claimed and marked its cattle. Each ranch had its own branding iron. This was a piece of iron shaped like a letter or symbol. While one cowboy heated the branding iron in a fire, other cowboys would have to get the longhorn. Needless to say, no cow liked being branded. While one cowboy threw a lariat around the cow's neck, another cowboy might slip one around its feet. It was a tricky job.

Once branded, the cattle were set loose to graze. After they got fat, they were driven up north to the markets and sold.

The cattle drive was the hardest part of being a cowboy. The drive could last for two to three months. The drives crossed the Indian Territory (now called Oklahoma). Usually the Texas cowboys gave some of their cattle to the Native Americans whose land they were crossing.

Most of the time, cowboys on a cattle drive fought with the weather. Rain and lightning storms were the biggest problem. Lightning caused stampedes. The cowboy's job was to stop them. To do this, he had to get in front of the stampeding cattle. If his horse slipped in the mud, he could be thrown and trampled to death. Also, the metal spurs he wore on his boots attracted lightning. Many cowboys were struck by lightning.

One of the first rodeo stars was an African-American cowboy named Bill Pickett. Pickett was a "bull-dogger." A bull-dogger was someone who could

wrestle a steer to the ground. Bill Pickett was the first and most famous person to do this dangerous feat.

Pickett was not by any means the only African-American cowboy. In the Old West, many cowboys were black. After slavery ended in 1865, many former slaves needed jobs. Because they could ride horses, many became cowboys.

Another famous African-American cowboy was Nat Love. He was a terrific rider and roper. He was also known for his wild stories. He claimed that he once rode 100 miles on a horse with no saddle. Like many tales from the Wild West, Nat's story is half-truth and half-fiction.

Nat Love was a real person, though, and a real cowboy. Real cowboys were different from what we know from the movies. They all had one thing in common, though—cattle.